# SYRACUSE BASKETBALL

Severna Park
Middle School
Media Center

## JOHN M. SHEA

rosen publishing's
rosen
central®
New York

*To my father, one of Canisius's great basketball players*

Published in 2014 by The Rosen Publishing Group, Inc.
29 East 21st Street, New York, NY 10010

**Library of Congress Cataloging-in-Publication Data**

Shea, John M.
Syracuse basketball/John M. Shea. — 1st ed. — New York : Rosen, c2014
        p. cm. — (America's most winning teams)
Includes bibliographical references and index.
ISBN: 978-1-4488-9407-9 (Library Binding)
ISBN: 978-1-4488-9440-6 (Paperback)
ISBN: 978-1-4488-9441-3 (6-pack)
1. Syracuse Orange (Basketball team)—Juvenile literature. 2. Syracuse University—Basketball—Juvenile literature. 3. Syracuse University—Basketball—History. 4. Syracuse Orange (Basketball team) —History. I. Title.
GV885.43.S95 .S54 2014

796.323'630974766

*Manufactured in the United States of America*

CPSIA Compliance Information: Batch #S13YA: For further information, contact Rosen Publishing, New York, New York, at 1-800-237-9932.

# CONTENTS

# INTRODUCTION

When discussing successful college men's basketball teams, it is nearly impossible not to bring up Syracuse University. The Orange is the fifth winningest men's team in Division I of the National Collegiate Athletic Association (NCAA). The team has won approximately 70 percent of all the games it has played in its long history. Syracuse has made more than thirty-five NCAA tournament appearances, including five Final Four contests. It has won three national championship titles.

Syracuse holds an NCAA Division I record for the most consecutive winning seasons. The team has not had a losing season since 1971, a trend continued by current coach Jim Boeheim. Boeheim has led the Orange to postseason tournament playoffs every year but one, including four runs to the NCAA Final Four and one NCAA championship title. He is also the NCAA's fastest winning coach, having won one hundred games in just four years.

The history of Syracuse basketball is a long and interesting one. The Orange did not begin as a winning team. Indeed, the team spent its first three years not only without a winning season but without a coach as well. When John A. R. Scott took on the coaching duties for basketball, he became the first of only seven coaches for the Orange during their entire existence. Scott won more games than he lost during

Brandon Triche (#20) and DaJuan Coleman (#32) exhibit skill, hard work, and teamwork—traits common among many Syracuse basketball players —in a game against the Villanova Wildcats.

his time as coach, which is a trend that every coach after him also followed.

The story of the Orange is a story of the talented coaches that led the team. It is a story of extraordinary players that will be remembered in the record books and in the minds of the fans. It is a story of teamwork because even the best players cannot single-handedly carry a team to victory. It is a story of a university in central New York that has left its mark on the sport of basketball forever.

# CHAPTER 1

# SYRACUSE TAKES TO THE COURT

At the end of the nineteenth century, Dr. James Naismith invented the game of basketball. Naismith taught physical education at the Young Men's Christian Association (YMCA) International Training School, now known as Springfield College, in Massachusetts. He wanted an indoor game that would keep his students entertained and active during the long winter months. He nailed peach baskets on either side of a gymnasium, and in December 1891, the first basketball game was played. The following month, Dr. Naismith published the rules of the game. Basketball quickly became popular at other colleges throughout the country.

## FIRST SEASONS

Less than ten years after the game was invented, Syracuse University (SU) formed a men's basketball team. This first team had eight players, including a team captain. There was no coach; the team captain was in charge. Fred Stensel was to be the team captain, but he became ill and was unable to play any of the games. Bill Lowe became captain in his place.

Syracuse's first game was played against Rensselaer Polytechnic Institute on January 5, 1901. Syracuse

James Naismith *(wearing a suit)* poses with the first basketball team in Springfield, Massachusetts, in 1891. Within a decade, basketball would become popular at many colleges, including Syracuse.

was defeated with a score of 21–8. SU went on to win its next two games against Cornell University and St. Lawrence University. However, the men lost their last game against St. John's Military Academy and finished their first season with a 2–2 record.

In the second season, they played a total of six games. As in the first season, they lost the first game to Rensselaer Polytechnic Institute and finished the season by winning half of the games. The third season, however, proved to be disastrous. Syracuse lost the first seven games of the season and finished with a 1–8 record.

# THE FIRST COACH

During the first three seasons, the team captain and the team manager shared coaching duties. Because of SU's losing record, it was felt that the team could benefit from a dedicated coach. Dr. John A. R. Scott, the athletics director for Syracuse, volunteered for the position. Scott coached the men's team from 1903 to 1911. The 1903–1904 season was a tough one. The team played nineteen games, including ten games within a two-week period. Despite this challenging schedule, Syracuse University achieved its first

## THE SYRACUSE ORANGE

According to Frank J. Marion, a Syracuse graduate from the class of 1890, the school colors were originally blue and pink. When he was a senior, Marion and some classmates decided these colors were not vibrant enough to represent the school, and they discussed changing the colors with school officials. Marion and his classmates originally suggested orange and olive green, as those were the colors representing the senior class. After doing some research, it was discovered that while some schools used orange in combination with other colors, no college used orange by itself. School officials enthusiastically voted to change SU's official color to orange.

Orange became not only the school's color but also the name of the school's athletic teams. Syracuse's men's basketball team became known as the Orangemen when Eddie Dollard began coaching. Later, the women's basketball team became known as the Orangewomen. In the summer of 2004, the names of all SU sports teams, both men's and women's, were changed to simply the Orange. Otto the Orange—a giant orange fruit with arms, legs, and a blue SU baseball cap—has been the official mascot since 1995.

Since its introduction, this mascot has had many nicknames, including "Clyde" and "Woody." In 1990, Syracuse cheerleaders nicknamed him "Otto," a name that has stuck to this day.

Syracuse University athletic director John A. R. Scott was the school's first men's basketball coach from 1903 to 1911.

winning season with an 11–8 record.

Part of this success was attributable to several great players. George Kirchgasser, Art Powell, George Redlein, and Frank "Max" Riehl had all played basketball together in high school and then for the Buffalo Germans (an Amateur Athletic Union team) before playing for SU. Known as the Buffalo Foursome, these players were the best scorers for the team. Along with teammate Eddie Dollard and team manager Charles Kinne, they were the first SU basketball players to be awarded varsity letters in April 1906.

Scott's tenure as coach was a largely successful one. He won 54 percent of the games he coached. During Scott's first five seasons, Syracuse had a winning record, but during the next three seasons, they started losing. In part, these defeats were caused by Syracuse losing some outstanding, high-scoring players, including the Buffalo Foursome. While SU had some fine players between 1908 and 1911, the team as a whole was not as strong or as well rounded as it was before.

# EDDIE DOLLARD

After losing his third season in a row, Scott stepped down from the coaching position and hired one of his former players, Edmund "Eddie" Dollard, to take his place. Dollard played guard between 1904 and 1908, and he was captain of the team during his senior year. The team record while he was playing was thirty-seven wins and sixteen losses.

Dollard was the Orangemen's first paid coach, and he led the team for thirteen seasons. He emphasized a solid defense and a strong passing game. Dollard's leadership paid off, as the Orangemen had winning seasons for the first eleven years he coached. They were undefeated at home for his first five seasons, and they had their first (and only) undefeated season in 1913–1914.

Part of the team's success was due to player Lewis "Lew" Castle. Castle was a well-rounded athlete. He played halfback in football, and his crew team won the Intercollegiate Rowing Association regatta. In addition, he was the student body president. But it was in basketball that Castle truly shined. He became SU's first Helms Foundation all-American player in 1912. He was the captain of the Orangemen during their undefeated season. He scored a total of 155 points that season, which accounted for 42 percent of the team's total points.

Eddie Dollard coached the Orangemen during another first for Syracuse—a national championship in 1917 –1918. An expert panel appointed by the Helms Foundation chose the team as the national champion for the season. Joseph Schwarzer, a center, was team captain that year. Schwarzer, who was studying law at SU, was another

# HOME COURTS

The first SU men's basketball game was played at the State Armory on January 5, 1901. In 1908, the Archbold Gymnasium was opened, giving the Orangemen a permanent place to call their home court. They would play there for nearly four decades until a fire nearly destroyed the whole building in 1947.

The team temporarily moved to the coliseum on the New York State Fairgrounds until their new home, the Manley Field House, was finished in 1962. The 1960s and 1970s were an exciting time for Syracuse fans because of extraordinary players such as Dave Bing and Dennis DuVal. The student sections were especially noisy, which caused some people to refer to this area as the Manley Field Zoo. This loud enthusiasm gave the Orangemen a strong home court advantage.

Tens of thousands of SU fans in blue and orange are a common sight at the Carrier Dome, Syracuse's home court since 1980.

The Manley Field House was lucky for the Orangemen, and from 1962 to 1980 they won 87 percent of their home games there. In 1980, the Orangemen moved to the Carrier Dome, which is the largest domed arena of any college. On February 27, 2010, the Carrier Dome set an NCAA attendance record of 34,616 spectators for a victory over Villanova.

well-rounded athlete. In addition to being the men's basketball captain, he was also the captain of the baseball and football teams.

The Orangemen won their first sixteen games that season before losing their last game to University of Pennsylvania, 17–16. Schwarzer had a total of 151 points that season, while fellow teammate John Cronauer had 141 points. Together, this accounted for more than 62 percent of the team's total points. The Helms Foundation named Joe Schwarzer an all-American.

Coach Dollard had consecutive wins for his first eleven seasons but then lost the next two seasons with 9–11 and 8–10 records. After this second straight losing season, Dollard stepped down from coaching. He left an impressive legacy, including a total of 152 wins and only 58 losses. He led the team to its only undefeated season and its first title as national champion.

# CHAPTER 2

# THE HIGHS AND LOWS

Lewis Andreas became coach after Eddie Dollard and held the position for twenty-five seasons. Like Dollard, Andreas was a Syracuse alumnus and a former athlete, although Andreas played football and baseball, not basketball. While coaching the men's basketball team, he also coached the men's football team from 1927–1929 and was the director of physical education and athletics until 1964.

Like Dollard before him, Andreas believed in a strong defense; he also encouraged a very physical game. However, Andreas did not plan a lot of plays for the team. Instead, he often let the players come up with their own strategies. Andreas thought that the positions of the players should be flexible. That is, a good forward should also be able to play the position of guard or center equally well in a game.

Andreas's defensive, physical, and flexible style paid off right away. After losing the final two seasons under Dollard, the Orangemen had a 15–2 winning season their first year under Andreas. The next season they had an even more impressive 19–1 record. The Helms Foundation named the team the national champion for the second time in 1926.

# WORLD WAR II

Andreas led the Orangemen through an impressive eighteen consecutive winning seasons from 1924 to 1942. This streak was broken during the 1942–1943 season. The United States was at war with the Axis powers, and many young men were drafted into or volunteered for the armed services. Ten of SU's basketball players left the team during the season to serve in the military, including several of the Orangemen's top scorers. Indeed, the last game of the season against Penn State was cancelled

Lewis Andreas was the head coach of the Orangemen from 1924 to 1950. He led the team through eighteen consecutive winning seasons and its first-ever postseason tournament.

because of the number of missing players, leaving Syracuse with an 8–10 record for the season.

Syracuse cancelled all school athletics the following season, 1943–1944. Basketball resumed for the 1944–1945 season. Most of the players were freshmen who had not been eligible to join the armed forces because of their ages. The Orangemen started the season winning their first five games, but their inexperience soon caught up with them. They finished the season with a 7–12 record, their worst since the 1910–1911 season.

# VIC HANSON AND THE THREE MUSKETEERS

From 1924 to 1927, Syracuse basketball featured the so-called Three Musketeers: Charlie Lee, Harlan "Gotch" Carr, and Vic Hanson. Each was a strong scorer, and their play together included great teamwork and excellent passing. Hanson was Syracuse's all-time leading scorer at the time. Opponents would often double-team Hanson to prevent him from shooting, which would free Lee or Carr for important scoring opportunities.

Hanson is among the best athletes in SU's history. He was named an all-American each of the three years he played basketball and football. He was captain of the basketball, football, and baseball teams. He was signed by the New York Yankees after graduation and played a season for its farm team. He returned to Syracuse to coach the football team in 1930, with his fellow Musketeer Gotch Carr serving as assistant coach.

Hanson is the only person inducted into both the Basketball Hall of Fame and the College Football Hall of Fame. In his honor, Syracuse University awards the Vic Hanson Medal of Excellence to individuals that have made an important contribution to college basketball.

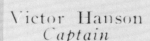

Victor Hanson
*Captain*

In the 1945–1946 season, many experienced players returned from the war to Syracuse and basketball. Billy "Bullet" Gabor was one of those experienced players. Having played in the 1942–1943 season, he became a bombardier during World War II. Upon his return, he led the team in scoring all three remaining years and set a new school record of 1,344 total points. The experience of Gabor and other veteran players allowed SU to bounce back from a losing streak with an impressive twenty-three wins—a new school record—and only four losses.

The 1945–1946 season was also notable as it marked the first time the Orangemen qualified to play in a postseason competition. The National Invitational Tournament (NIT) invited Syracuse to play Muhlenburg College in the first round. Muhlenburg proved to be a talented team, and the Orangemen did not score as well as they had in the regular season. Syracuse lost to Muhlenburg 47–41.

Syracuse returned to the NIT at the end of the 1949–1950 season, after achieving an 18–9 record. The first round was played against Long Island University, which was favored to win. However, the Orangemen surprised the crowds at Madison Square Garden when they defeated LIU 80–52. The next round pitted Syracuse against Bradley University, which was ranked number one that year. This time Syracuse lost, 78–66, and was eliminated from the tournament after the second round.

Lew Andreas retired as the men's basketball coach in 1950 to concentrate on his role as athletics director. He left behind an impressive legacy of 358 game wins and 134 losses, winning nearly three-quarters of the games he coached. He had twenty-two winning seasons, including eighteen in a row. Under his leadership, the Orangemen

## POSTSEASON TOURNAMENTS

Before 1937, the Helms Athletic Foundation, a group of sport experts, picked the basketball team that it considered to be the best of the year and awarded the team the title of Helms National Champion. In 1938, the National Invitational Tournament (NIT) began as a chance for some of the best teams in the nation to compete with each other at Madison Square Garden in New York City. A year later, the National Collegiate Athletic Association (NCAA), which sets standards and rules for college sports, began its own postseason tournaments.

There was competition between the NIT and the NCAA as to which winner was truly considered the national champion. Many Eastern schools, including Syracuse, preferred NIT tournaments because the games were played closer to home. However, the NCAA's influence over college sports eventually ensured that its tournament was considered the important one. Invitations to play in the NIT are now for those teams that do not qualify to play the NCAA tournament.

Syracuse University has been part of the Big East Conference of the NCAA since 1979. As of July 2013, however, it will join the Atlantic Coast Conference.

were recognized as Helms Foundation National Champions once and made it to the NIT postseason tournament twice.

# MARC GULEY

Marc Guley, an assistant coach under Andreas, took over coaching duties when Andreas stepped down. Born in Czechoslovakia, Guley played guard for the Orangemen between 1933 and 1936 and was the team captain his senior year.

Guley's time as coach started well. The team finished the season with a 16–9 record. That qualified them for a new tournament—the National Campus Tournament. Syracuse beat the University of Toledo in the first round and the University of Utah in the second round. For the third and final round, the Orangemen faced Bradley University, the host of the tournament and the team that had them during their last NIT tournament game. The game started badly, with Syracuse scoreless as Bradley shot the first eighteen points. Eventually, Syracuse rallied and beat the tournament favorite by one point, 76–75.

Thanks to talented players such as the record-breaking Vinnie Cohen, Syracuse qualified to play in the NCAA tournament for the first time in 1957.

The team did not have another postseason tournament appearance until the 1956–1957 season. That season the team had a lot of experienced and talented players, including forward Vinnie Cohen, who was averaging 24.2 points a game. Cohen was the first Syracuse player to score more than 600 points in a season. Syracuse finished the season with a 16–6 record and qualified for the NCAA postseason tournament for the first time. A hard-earned victory against Connecticut advanced the Orangemen to the second round, where they beat Lafayette in a close game. In the third round (known as the "Elite Eight"), they lost 67–58 to the number-one ranked North Carolina, which would go on to win the championship that year.

Despite this great accomplishment, the team began to fall apart afterward. Even with some talented players, Syracuse struggled to win for the next several seasons. During the 1960–1961 season, the team found it difficult to score, and it won only four of its twenty-three games. The next season was even worse: the Orangemen lost the first twenty-two games of the season. Combined with the losses from the previous season, this was a twenty-seven-game losing streak, an NCAA record at the time. The team won its last two games to finish what still ranks as the worst season in SU's history.

When that season was 0–16, Marc Guley announced that he would step down from coaching. Many consider him to be the worst coach in SU basketball history because he led the team through its worst season. He had only six wins out of the last forty-seven games of his final seasons. Still, Syracuse had winning seasons seven out of the twelve seasons he coached, and his team won more than 51 percent of the total games played. He also led the team to its first postseason tournament championship and to an impressive showing at its first NCAA appearance.

# CHAPTER 3

# THE ORANGE REBOUNDS TO VICTORY

Fred Lewis took over the coaching position in 1962. Lewis was a talented basketball player, having played for Long Island University and Eastern Kentucky University. He also played professional basketball and was named Rookie of the Year while playing for the Sheboygan Red Skins in 1947. He coached basketball at the University of Southern Mississippi before coming to Syracuse.

## LEWIS TURNS THE TEAM AROUND

Fred Lewis was a very demanding coach. He expected his players to work hard. He emphasized a quick-paced game in which the players did a lot of running and passing to keep their opponents off-balance. A favorite trick of his was to start the game with reserve players. When the opposing team's

Fred Lewis's experience as a basketball player and his demanding expectations of his players brought the team from its worst losing streak to postseason playoffs in just two years.

## DAVID BING

David Bing is considered one of the greatest players in Syracuse basketball history. When he played on the freshman team, sometimes fans would show up to watch him play and then leave before the varsity team played. When he joined the varsity team, the team's record jumped from 8–13 the prior year to 22–6. In his final year, Bing was fifth in the nation for scoring (28.4 points per game), an SU record. He also scored a total of 1,883 points while at Syracuse, breaking a record previously held by Billy "Bullet" Gabor.

At David Bing's Hall of Fame induction, legendary player Oscar Robertson said, "Dave is the perfect example of professionalism, class, dignity, and humanity. He cares. He gets involved with the world."

Bing was drafted in the NBA upon graduation. He earned Rookie of the Year his first year and led the NBA in scoring his second year. Both the Detroit Pistons and Syracuse University retired his jersey number in his honor. Bing was inducted into the Basketball Hall of Fame in 1990. That same year, he started a multimillion-dollar steel company. He developed a love for Detroit, and he helped run a campaign to save the athletics programs in Detroit's public schools. In a special election in 2009, Bing became mayor of Detroit.

top players would get tired, he would then play his own well-rested top players.

Lewis also worked hard to recruit talented players to the team. He brought in players such as David Bing, Jim Boeheim, and Chuck Richards to help lead the Orangemen from a record losing season to postseason playoffs within a few short seasons. In 1963–1964, just two years after the 2–22 finish, the Orangemen finished 17–8, their best season in seven years. They qualified for the NIT but lost to New York University in the first round.

In the 1965–1966 season, the Orangemen reached a new high. Led by seniors Bing and Boeheim, the team averaged ninety-nine points per game, which was a new NCAA record at the time. Bing scored forty-five points in one game, setting an SU record. The Orangemen finished the regular season with a 22–5 record and qualified for the NCAA tournament. They defeated Davidson College in the first round but lost to Duke in the Sweet Sixteen.

Lewis left Syracuse after six years to take a coaching position in California. In the short time he was there, however, he led the Orangemen from their worst season to three appearances at a postseason tournament. Four of the six years were winning seasons, and he won 91 (61.5 percent) of the 148 games he coached.

## ROY DANFORTH

Roy Danforth had played for Southern Mississippi while Fred Lewis was coaching there. He became an assistant coach for the Syracuse varsity team under Lewis in 1964. He was also the freshman basketball coach. He had a 57–8 record for the four years he coached the freshmen team, including a 15–1 record during his last year. He took over coaching duties of the varsity team when Lewis left in 1968.

Roy Danforth outlines a play against Kansas State during the 1975 NCAA playoffs. Syracuse beat Kansas in overtime, bringing the team to the Final Four for the first time.

Danforth's coaching was characterized by strong defensive plays that gave the opponents little opportunity to shoot or pass the ball. Danforth was also known for his showmanship. He would try to get the crowd excited and loud. For example, he encouraged Dennis DuVal, an excellent shooter, to make trick shots to entertain the crowds before home games.

Danforth's first two seasons were not spectacular: the Orangemen finished 9–16 the first season and 12–12 the second season. But starting in the third season, Danforth led the Orangemen to six consecutive tournament appearances. In the 1970–1971 season, the Orangemen finished with a 19–6 record. They lost in the first round of the NIT postseason tournament. The next year they did better, achieving a 21–5 season record and advancing to the second round of the NIT playoffs.

Thanks in part to the high-scoring DuVal, Syracuse continued winning games, and the next season (1972–1973), the team qualified for a playoff spot in the NCAA tournament. This was the first time the Orangemen had the chance to play in a postseason tournament three years in a row, and only the third time they qualified for the prestigious NCAA tournament. After winning the first-round game by a single point, Syracuse lost the next round against the University of Maryland. The following season, the Orangemen once again qualified for a NCAA playoff spot. This time, however, they were eliminated in the first round in an overtime loss against Oral Roberts University.

The 1974–1975 season marked the "Drive for Five," an attempt to make a fifth consecutive postseason tournament appearance. The team and the fans knew it was not going to be easy, especially since one of Syracuse's best players, DuVal, had just graduated. But there were other strong players,

# "SWEET D" DUVAL

Dennis "Sweet D" DuVal was an outstanding guard on Syracuse's varsity team from 1971 to 1974. He led the team in scoring during his junior and senior years, contributing about twenty points each game. His career point total of 1,504 was second only to David Bing. He helped bring the Orangemen to the NCAA tournament twice in a row during his final two years.

DuVal is remembered not only for the points he made but also for how he shot them. He was a flashy player who liked to show off. Coach Danforth saw DuVal goofing off with some trick shots,

DuVal made a name for himself as one of the top scorers in SU's history. He later made history by becoming Syracuse's first African American chief of police.

and the two came up with an idea. DuVal would perform his trick shots during the warm-ups before the home games, while Danforth would lead the crowd in cheers.

DuVal played professional basketball for four years and then returned to Syracuse to become a police officer. In 1990 he became deputy police chief, and in 2001 he became the chief of police.

In 1984 DuVal was awarded the prestigious Vic Hanson Medal of Excellence. In 1994 he was inducted into the Syracuse Hall of Fame.

such as cocaptains Rudy Hackett and Jimmy Lee, that gave them confidence. That confidence paid off, as the Orangemen won eleven of their first thirteen games. They suffered some losses halfway through the season due to problems with their teamwork. However, they were able to pull together and win their final games and once again earn an NCAA playoff position. The first three rounds were characterized by very close victories, including two overtime games. Syracuse advanced to the Final Four for the first time. The Orangemen lost to the second-ranked Kentucky Wildcats, 95–79.

Danforth brought Syracuse to the NCAA one more time the next season, although the Orangemen were eliminated in the first round. Danforth left at the end of the season to coach Tulane University's basketball team. During his eight years of coaching at Syracuse, his only losing season was his first one, and he won 148 (68 percent) of the 218 games he coached. Danforth started a consecutive winning-season streak that continues to this day. He brought the team to six consecutive postseason tournaments, including four consecutive NCAA appearances and its first Final Four appearance. He started a streak of consecutive postseason tournament appearances that would last for twenty-two years.

# CHAPTER 4

# THE BOEHEIM ERA

**P**erhaps no one is more associated with Syracuse basketball than Jim Boeheim. As a player, he was cocaptain and roommate of the great Dave Bing. Upon graduation, he played minor league basketball before returning to Syracuse as a graduate assistant and then an assistant coach, under Roy Danforth. When Danforth left for Tulane University, Syracuse officials considered coaches from other schools as his replacement. However, a group of former Orangemen strongly recommended Boeheim for the job as head coach. The school officials finally agreed, and Jim Boeheim became head coach in 1976.

The Orangemen succeeded under Boeheim's leadership right away. They won one hundred games within his first four years, a record for an NCAA Division I coach. Part of this success was because of two outstanding players: Louis Orr and Roosevelt Bouie. These two players were among Boeheim's first recruits to the team. Together they were known as "The Bouie 'n' Louie Show."

Boeheim continued Danforth's streak of qualifying for postseason playoffs during his first sixteen seasons. Fourteen of those seasons would see the Orangemen play in the NCAA tournament. The team routinely

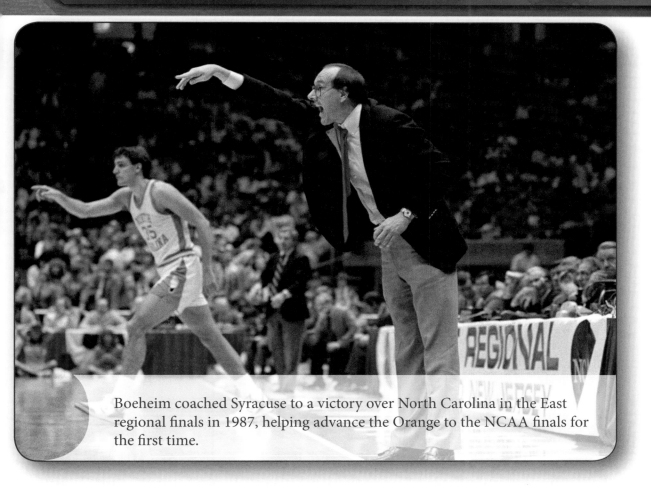

Boeheim coached Syracuse to a victory over North Carolina in the East regional finals in 1987, helping advance the Orange to the NCAA finals for the first time.

won twenty or more games each season, but Boeheim had earned a reputation for not being able to win important games. The team never advanced past the Sweet Sixteen during that time.

## SO CLOSE

Severna Park Middle School Media Center

That changed during the 1986–1987 season. Not much was expected from the Orangemen that year, as several great players had graduated the year before. However, a new combination of talent, including freshman Derrick Coleman and the more experienced cocaptains Greg Monroe and Howard Triche, soon showed everyone the Orangemen were the team to beat. They won the Big East season championship and qualified for the NCAA tournament.

Syracuse beat Georgia Southern University, Western Kentucky University, and University of Florida in the first three rounds. SU finally made it past the Sweet Sixteen but now faced the top seed, North Carolina. The Orangemen beat the Tar Heels 79–75, thanks in part to Rony Seikaly, a center who had been improving all season and who scored twenty-six points in the game. After defeating Providence College, Syracuse faced Indiana University in the finals. It was a very close game. The Orangemen led 73–72 with less than thirty seconds left in the game. However, a two-point shot by Indiana in the last seconds of the game gave the victory—and the NCAA championship title—to the Hoosiers.

## BATTLING BACK

Syracuse continued to play strong in the following years. Between 1987 and 1995, Syracuse was the Big East season champion twice, and the Big East tournament champion another two times. The team also qualified for the NCAA playoffs every year except 1993, when it was banned from participating in the tournament for violating NCAA recruitment rules. Some amazing players were donning orange jerseys at this time, such as Derrick "D.C." Coleman. During high school in Detroit, Coleman learned from the great Dave Bing, and he went on to set a new record for most career points. That record lasted only a few years, until Lawrence Moten (referred to as "Poetry in Moten" for how easy and graceful he made his games look) set a new record of 2,334 total points. Moten's record still stands today.

When SU retired Derrick Coleman's number 44 jersey in 2006, he said fondly, "I had more fun playing college basketball here at Syracuse University than I ever had playing in the NBA."

Despite these outstanding players and the Orangemen's domination of the Big East, after 1987 they didn't advance past the Elite Eight for the next eight seasons. This changed in the 1995–1996 season. John Wallace, a high-scoring forward and well-rounded player, was eligible for the NBA that season, but he decided at the last minute to stay at Syracuse to finish his senior year. He averaged more than twenty-two points per game that season. In the NCAA tournament, the Orangemen readily won their first two rounds but faced difficulty against the Georgia Bulldogs, finally winning in overtime by two points. Syracuse then defeated Kansas and Mississippi State to advance to the NCAA finals against the top-ranked Kentucky Wildcats. The Orangemen shot well during that game but gave away too many turnovers, which cost them. They lost to the Wildcats, 76–67.

# PURSUING THE BIG WIN

Syracuse struggled over the next six seasons. Although the Orangemen continued to have winning seasons, they did not qualify for the NCAA tournament twice during this time. When they did qualify, they did not advance past the Sweet Sixteen. Their luck did not seem to be improving at the start of the 2002–2003 season, when Billy Edelin, a promising new recruit, was suspended by the NCAA for playing in a church league the previous summer.

But as the season progressed, it became apparent that something special was happening. Two freshmen, Carmelo "Melo" Anthony and Gerry McNamara, quickly became recognized as outstanding players. As point guard, McNamara made incredible shots. He set a Big East record for making more than 90 percent of his free throws. Impressively,

# CARMELO "MELO" ANTHONY

"Melo" is an appropriate nick-name for this easygoing, ever-smiling forward. From the start of his only season (2002–2003) at Syracuse, he made a name for himself by scoring more than twenty-five points in each of his first three games. He was also an excellent team player and encouraged other Orange-men to play bigger roles in games. That hard work by mul-tiple players was what allowed the Orangemen to advance through the NCAA tournament and win the championship that season. Anthony was named the tournament's Most Valuable Player, and the Big East's Rookie of the Year.

Anthony left after his fresh-man year to play in the NBA. During his first year with the team, the Denver Nuggets went from the worst team in the league to earning a playoff spot. He was traded to the New York Knicks in 2011.

Anthony was part of the U.S. men's Olympic team that won the bronze medal in 2004. He was also on the 2008 and 2012 teams, which each won gold medals. He set a U.S. Olympic team record for the most points in a single game (thirty-seven) during the 2012 match against Nigeria.

The ever-smiling Carmelo Anthony helped lead the Orange to its first NCAA championship title in 2003. His number 15 jersey was retired in February 2013.

he made about a third of his three-point shots as well. McNamara would finish his stay at Syracuse as the fourth all-time leading scorer.

The Orangemen lost their first game that season, but then won the next eleven in a row. Although Anthony and McNamara were emerging as stars, these games were more notable for their teamwork. Every night, another teammate would step up and help carry the team to victory. Hakim "Hak Attack" Warrick, a 6-foot, 8-inch (203 cm) sophomore, put a lot of defensive pressure on his opponents, and his vertical leaps and dunks sometimes earned him twenty or more points a game. The team's perseverance was also noticeable: that season the Orangemen won fifteen games after being behind in the second half.

The Orangemen swept through the NCAA playoffs, beating their opponents by ten or more points in all but one of the games. The 2003 NCAA finals were held in New

On January 2, 2013, Boeheim became the NCAA's second winningest coach, overtaking coaching legend Bobby Knight.

Orleans, the same city where Syracuse had lost to Indiana in the NCAA finals of 1987. Syracuse played exceptionally well during the first half of the game, with McNamara scoring eighteen points from three-point shots alone. However, the Kansas Jayhawks fought back in the second half and came within three points of Syracuse with just seconds left in the game. Mike Lee of the Jayhawks attempted a three-point shot that would have forced the game into overtime. However, with his tremendous vertical leap, Hakim Warrick blocked the shot, allowing the Orangemen to win the game and their first-ever NCAA championship.

# AFTER THE CHAMPIONSHIP

In the seasons that followed, the team did not reach the level of success that it had in 2003. Anthony left to play for the NBA after his freshman year, leaving McNamara and Warrick to lead the team. In the first round of the NCAA tournament in 2004, McNamara scored forty-three points, but Syracuse was eliminated in the Sweet Sixteen. The following year, McNamara fell into a slump and was not making the impressive shots he had during his first two years. Warrick continued to play well and helped lead Syracuse to the Big East tournament champion title in 2005. Warrick earned the tournament's Most Valuable Player and the Big East Player of the Year. However, the team was eliminated from the NCAA tournament in the first round.

In the ten years since the NCAA championship, the Orange made eight more NCAA postseason tournament appearances. The team made it to the Sweet Sixteen three times, to the Elite Eight once, and to the Final Four once, during the 2012–2013 season. For the two seasons that Syracuse did not qualify for the NCAA tournament (2006–2007 and 2007–2008), the team did qualify for the NIT and made it to the quarterfinals each time. Syracuse was also the Big East season champion twice and the Big East tournament champion twice.

The success of Syracuse basketball is partly attributable to the leadership of Jim Boeheim. With victories in about 75 percent of games played, he is the winningest coach not only in Syracuse basketball history but also in Big East history. This record also ranks him as one of the winningest coaches in NCAA history, behind only Mike Krzyzewski of Duke University. Boeheim was assistant coach to the United States men's Olympic basketball teams of 2008 and 2012; both teams won gold medals. It is little wonder that few people embody the spirit of Syracuse basketball as much as Jim Boeheim.

## TIMELINE

**January 5, 1901**  Syracuse plays its first game against Rensselaer Polytechnic Institute, losing 21–8.

**1903**  John A. R. Scott becomes the first coach of men's basketball, and the team has its first winning season.

**1911**  Eddie Dollard becomes head coach.

**1913–1914**  The Orangemen have an undefeated season.

**1918**  The Orangemen are named Helms Foundation National Champions.

**1924**  Lew Andreas becomes head coach.

**1926**  The Orangemen are again named Helms Foundation National Champions.

**1943–1944**  Syracuse University cancels all sports due to World War II.

**1946**  Syracuse plays in the NIT tournament for the first time.

**1950**  Marc Guley becomes head coach.

**1951**  The Orangemen win the National Campus Tournament.

**1957**  Syracuse plays in the NCAA tournament for the first time.

**1962**  Fred Lewis becomes head coach; the team moves into Manley Field House.

**1968**  Roy Danforth becomes head coach.

**1970–1971**  The Orangemen begin their winning-season streak.

**1975**  The Orangemen make their first Final Four appearance.

**1976**  Jim Boeheim becomes head coach.

**1979–1980**  Jim Boeheim becomes the fastest coach to reach one hundred wins.

**1980**  The Orangemen move into the Carrier Dome.

**1987**  The Orangemen are the NCAA championship runners-up.

**1996**  The Orangemen are again the NCAA championship runners-up.

**2003**  Syracuse wins the NCAA championship.

**2010**  The Carrier Dome sets new NCAA basketball attendance record.

**July 2013**  Syracuse joins the Atlantic Coast Conference (ACC).

# GLOSSARY

**alumnus**  A former student, usually a graduate, of a particular school.

**bombardier**  A crew member of a military aircraft that releases bombs.

**center**  Usually the tallest member of the team, this player's responsibility is to both shoot and defend close to the basket.

**collegiate**  Having to do with a college or university.

**consecutive**  Following another in a continuous and unbroken manner.

**defense**  The action or role of defending the basket against the opposition.

**draft**  A procedure whereby sports players are made available for selection by professional teams.

**forward**  A position in basketball usually played close to the basket. Forwards tend to be good shooters and rebounders.

**guard**  A position in basketball usually played farther away from the basket than the other positions. Guards are usually quick and excel at making long-distance shots.

**legacy**  Something from the past that is left for future generations.

**perseverance**  The act of continuing a course of action even though it appears difficult.

**point guard**  A position in basketball that controls the offense for the team. The point guard is usually the team's best ball handler and passer.

**prestigious**  Having an excellent reputation; well-respected.

**tenure**  The period of time for which someone holds a particular job.

**tournament**  A sporting competition in which competitors play a series of games to decide the winner.

**varsity**  The main team representing a college, school, or club in competition.

**vibrant**  Bright and striking.

## Atlantic Coast Conference (ACC)

4512 Weybridge Lane
Greensboro, NC 27407
(336) 854-8787
Web site: http://www.theacc.com
The home of Syracuse University athletics from summer 2013 on, the ACC provides statistics and other information about members of this conference.

## Big East Conference

15 Park Row West
Providence, RI 02903
(401) BIG-EAST [244-3278]
Web site: http://www.bigeast.org
The home of Syracuse University athletics until 2013, the Big East includes some of the best collegiate basketball teams in the NCAA.

## Greater Syracuse Sports Hall of Fame

1 Tex Simone Drive
Syracuse, NY 13208
(315) 657-3718
Web site: http://www.syracusehalloffame.com
Every year, the Greater Syracuse Sports Hall of Fame recognizes outstanding athletes from Central New York, including many athletes and coaches from Syracuse University.

## National Basketball Association (NBA)

645 Fifth Avenue
New York, NY 10022
(212) 407-8000

Web site: http://www.nba.com
The NBA is the major professional basketball league of the United States. On its Web site, fans of Syracuse basketball can follow favorite players who went on to play professional basketball.

### National Collegiate Athletic Association (NCAA)

700 W. Washington Street
P.O. Box 6222
Indianapolis, IN 46206-6222
(317) 917-6222
Web site: http://www.ncaa.org
The NCAA oversees and regulates the athletics programs of colleges and universities. It organizes the postseason basketball tournament every year.

### Syracuse University

900 South Crouse Avenue
Syracuse, NY 13244
(315) 443-1870
Web site: http://www.syr.edu
Located in central New York State, this 140-year-old university has strong programs in both athletics and academics.

# WEB SITES

Due to the changing nature of Internet links, Rosen Publishing has developed an online list of Web sites related to the subject of this book. This site is updated regularly. Please use this link to access the list:

http://www.rosenlinks.com/AMWT/SCBB

# FOR FURTHER READING

Augustyn, Adam, ed. *The Britannica Guide to Basketball* (World of Sports). New York, NY: Britannica Educational Publishing in association with Rosen Educational Services, 2011.

Baker, Mark Allen. *Basketball History in Syracuse: Hoops Roots.* Charleston, SC: History Press, 2010.

Bekkering, Annalise. *NCAA Basketball* (Pro Sports Championships). New York, NY: AV2 by Weigl, 2013.

Feinstein, John. *Last Dance: Behind the Scenes at the Final Four.* Boston, MA: Little, Brown, 2007.

Gifford, Clive. *Basketball* (Personal Best). New York, NY: PowerKids Press, 2009.

Hager, Tom. *The Ultimate Book of March Madness: The Players, Games, and Cinderellas That Captivated a Nation.* Minneapolis, MN: MVP Books, 2012.

Kelly, Greg, ed. *The College Basketball Book.* New York, NY: Sports Illustrated, 2011.

MacRae, Sloan. *Carmelo Anthony* (Sports Heroes). New York, NY: PowerKids Press, 2012.

Pitoniak, Scott. *Color Him Orange: The Jim Boeheim Story.* Chicago, IL: Triumph Books, 2011.

Porterfield, Jason. *Basketball in the ACC: Atlantic Coast Conference* (Inside Men's College Basketball). New York, NY: Rosen Central, 2008.

Porterfield, Jason. *Basketball in the Big East Conference* (Inside Men's College Basketball). New York, NY: Rosen Central, 2008.

Rippey, Tom P., and Paul F. Wilson. *Orangeology Trivia Challenge: Syracuse Orange Basketball*. Lewis Center, OH: Kick the Ball Ltd., 2009.

Schulte, Mary E. *The Final Four: All About College Basketball's Biggest Event* (Winner Takes All). Mankato, MN: Capstone Press, 2013.

Steward, Mark, and Matt Zeysing. *The Syracuse Orange.* Chicago, IL: Norwood House Press, 2011.

Waters, Mike. *Syracuse University Basketball Vault: The History of the Orange*. Atlanta, GA: Whitman Publishing, 2009.

Wilner, Barry, and Ken Rappoport. *The Big Dance: The Story of the NCAA Basketball Tournament*. Lanham, MD: Taylor Trade Publishing, 2012.

# BIBLIOGRAPHY

Associated Press. "Jackson, Onuaku Help Orange Drop Wildcats in Front of Record Crowd." ESPN.com, February 27, 2010. Retrieved October 10, 2012 (http://sports.espn.go.com/ncb/recap?gameId=300580183).

Crouthamel, Jake. "A Big East History & Retrospective (Part I)." SUAthletics.com, December 8, 2000. Retrieved October 10, 2012 (http://www.suathletics.com/sports/2001/8/8/history.aspx).

ESPN.com. "Dr. James Naismith—The Inventor of Basketball—NBA Topics." May 20, 2011. Retrieved October 10, 2012 (http://espn.go.com/nba/topics/_/page/james-naismith).

FOXSports.com. "Top 10 Winningest D-I Men's College Basketball Coaches." September 12, 2012. Retrieved October 10, 2012 (http://msn.foxsports.com/collegebasketball/lists/All-time-top-10-winningest-D-I-college-basketball-coaches-111511).

Greater Syracuse Sports Hall of Fame. "Vic Hanson." Retrieved October 10, 2012 (http://syracusehalloffame.com/pages/inductees/1987/vic_hanson.html).

Moore, Matt. "Carmelo Anthony Sets U.S. Men's Olympic Record for Points." CBSSports.com, August 2, 2012. Retrieved October 10, 2012 (http://www.cbssports.com/nba/blog/eye-on-basketball/19713912/carmelo-anthony-sets-us-mens-olympic-record-for-points).

National Collegiate Athletic Association (NCAA). "2010–11 NCAA Men's Basketball Records—Division I Records." Retrieved October 10, 2012 (http://fs.ncaa.org/Docs/stats/m_basketball_RB/2011/D1.pdf).

NBA.com. "Dave Bing Bio." Retrieved October 10, 2012 (http://www.nba.com/history/players/bing_bio.html).

Snyder, Bob, ed. *Syracuse Basketball: A Century of Memories.* Champaign, IL: Sports Publishing, 1999.

Syracuse University Archives. "Syracuse University Buildings: Archbold Gymnasium." Retrieved October 10, 2012 (http://archives.syr.edu/buildings/archbold.html).

Syracuse University Archives. "Syracuse University History: Why Orange?" Retrieved October 10, 2012 (http://archives.syr.edu/history/orange.html).

Syracuse University Athletics. "Manley Field House History." SUAthletics.com. Retrieved October 10, 2012 (http://www.suathletics.com/sports/2010/10/21/GEN_1021102213.aspx?id=7323).

Waters, Mike. *The Orangemen: Syracuse University Men's Basketball* (Images of Sports). Charleston, SC: Arcadia, 2002.

# INDEX

# ABOUT THE AUTHOR

A native of western New York, John Shea is an ardent supporter of that great state, including its history, its ecology, and its sports teams. He played basketball in high school and gets infected with March Madness each year. When he is not writing, he can usually be found loudly cheering for the Buffalo Sabres.

# PHOTO CREDITS

Cover, pp. 1, 5, 6, 14, 21 (top), 28 Nate Shron/Getty Images; back cover (hoop) Mike Flippo/Shutterstock.com; p. 4 Marc Squire/Getty Images; p. 7 Hulton Archive/Getty Images; p. 9 Ezra Shaw/Getty Images; pp. 10, 15, 16, 19, 21 (bottom), 22 Collegiate Images/Getty Images; p. 12 Fred Vuich /Sports Illustrated/Getty Images; p. 24 James Drake/Sports Illustrated/Getty Images; pp. 26, 29, 31 © AP Images; p. 33 John Biever/Sports Illustrated/Getty Images; pp. 34–35 Chris Chambers/Getty Images; multiple interior page borders and boxed text backgrounds (basketball) Mark Cinotti/Shutterstock.com; back cover and multiple interior pages background (abstract pattern) © iStockphoto.com/Che McPherson.

Designer: Nicole Russo; Editor: Andrea Sclarow Paskoff; Photo Researcher: Marty Levick